T0194985

A ROSE AMONG ASHES

One Woman's Journey through Abortion

TAMARA S. WEBB

WESTBOW
PRESS®
A DIVISION OF THOMAS NELSON
& ZONDERVAN

This book is a work of non-fiction. Unless otherwise noted, the author
and the publisher make no explicit guarantees as to the accuracy of
the information contained in this book and in some cases, names of
people and places have been altered to protect their privacy.

WestBow Press books may be ordered through booksellers or by contacting:

WestBow Press
A Division of Thomas Nelson & Zondervan
1663 Liberty Drive
Bloomington, IN 47403
www.westbowpress.com
1 (866) 928-1240

Because of the dynamic nature of the Internet, any web addresses or
links contained in this book may have changed since publication and
may no longer be valid. The views expressed in this work are solely those
of the author and do not necessarily reflect the views of the publisher,
and the publisher hereby disclaims any responsibility for them.

Any people depicted in stock imagery provided by Getty Images are
models, and such images are being used for illustrative purposes only.
Certain stock imagery © Getty Images.

Scripture taken from the King James Version of the Bible.

ISBN: 978-1-9736-9047-4 (sc)
ISBN: 978-1-9736-9049-8 (hc)
ISBN: 978-1-9736-9048-1 (e)

Library of Congress Control Number: 2020907726

Print information available on the last page.

WestBow Press rev. date: 5/19/2020

For baby Anthony

To my Savior, thank you for rescuing me from myself.

To my family, thank you for walking this journey with me. This book has truly been a family project.

To my Honeybear, Jim, you walked the hard road with me before healing ever came. You loved me when I did not love myself.

To my four daughters—Kris, Trish, Angel, and Jess—I love all of you more than any of you will ever comprehend. You are my girls!

To my prayer warriors, this book will accomplish what God has intended because of your faithfulness in prayer. Thank you for interceding!

CONTENTS

Scriptures:

Unless otherwise indicated, scripture quotations are from the King James Version of the Bible.

A special thanks to Eaton Floral of Eaton, Ohio, for their contribution.

INTRODUCTION

This story is about a very powerful experience between two strangers and the divine intervention of God that would change their lives forever.

What began as a simple mistake became the biggest blessing.

This "mistake" was a text meant for a friend to receive, but as God would have it, a stranger received the message instead.

A light was about to break through the darkness—for them both. While one of them would learn how much God cares about her and every detail of her life, it taught the other one that their potential goes beyond her past—a past that you, the reader, will soon discover.

This transformational story will bring tears to your eyes, understanding to your mind, and grace to your heart.

Give yourself permission to hurt and to heal as you read this story, because you will not be the same hereafter.

Perhaps while reading you feel the need to do some unpacking of your own experiences or feelings. Or maybe you do not feel like you have someone in whom you can confide; a safe place is provided at the end of every chapter for you to pour out your heart. Provided at the start of each safe place is a writing prompt. If you need it, use it; if not, just write what is on your heart. Make it what you need it to be!

My sincere hope is that you begin the journey of healing as you take the time to read and respond honestly and that when you do, you receive a peace sweeter than you have ever known.

CHAPTER 1

Lord, Here Am I

For many are called, but few are chosen.

—Matthew 22:14

Have you ever been your own judge, jury, and prosecuting attorney? I have, and I sentenced my life to guilt without parole. I did not think I was worthy of anything or able to do anything of any importance. But somehow, someway, God intervened.

It may be common knowledge to you that God has a purpose for your life and that if you are still breathing you can still walk in it. But that was a hard pill for me to swallow under my guilt sentence. So when God began teaching me that each of us has a calling in life to be an intricate part of his kingdom, I thought I could never measure up.

On my own, that was true. To fulfill that calling, I

had to make a choice. If God was going to choose me for a task in his kingdom, I must align myself with his Son, Jesus, to walk the path that he desired for me.

Unfortunately, the path does not always come easy. Sometimes, his ways and his timing do not feel convenient or comfortable at all. There are times that his will may require you or me to do something very hard or something so scary our hearts race. But if we will trust him and choose to answer the call with a simple, "Lord, here am I," the next step will come.

While some calls may not feel significant to you personally, there are many times when God will call you to a task that will be monumental; it will change your life forever.

This story begins with my answer to a call in 2012 that did just that—it changed my life forever.

It was a late summer night around eleven o'clock. My husband and I were in bed watching television when I received an alert on my phone. At first, I was not going to check it, but something urged me not to ignore it. So I grabbed my phone. It was a text message.

After reading the initial text, I thought it was a message from one of my brothers. But with just a few exchanges, I realized that the sender was not one of my brothers. I did not know this person, and I did not know if the sender deliberately texted a stranger or if it was an accident.

However, it was apparent that this person was in a seemingly very dark and lonely place and in need of guidance. Before I could even open up to this stranger with, "I'm a pastor's wife …," I became a sounding board.

The person on the other end was a high-fashion female model aspiring to fit the mold of physical perfection as expected in the modeling industry. Only, she had a problem.

She further expressed that she felt she could talk to me because we did not know each other personally. Because I did not know her, she knew that I could listen and respond without bias. Continuing, she revealed that she was pregnant and concerned about her future.

In her mind, working in an industry of *perfection* did not leave room for pregnancy scars. She did not know what step to take next. But I knew mine. It was to say, "Lord, here am I."

Then, my next step would be to share my story with her. You see, it was no coincidence that this text came to my phone on that night. God was intervening on her behalf but undoubtedly on my behalf as well.

Had she not texted, and the Lord not urged me, this story may still be unwritten. But by the grace of God, both of our stories will go on for his glory alone.

A SAFE PLACE FOR YOUR THOUGHTS ...

If you knew something in your past would help someone else, would you share it to help them, even if it was shameful? If yes, what experience came to mind? If no, why not?

_____

_____

_____

_____

_____

_____

_____

_____

_____

CHAPTER 2

Life Choices

The thief cometh not, but for to steal, and to kill,
and to destroy: I am come that they might have
life, and that they might have it more abundantly.

—John 10:10

The young woman I was speaking to through text messages was only twenty-one—an age I remember far too well. It was a time that changed my life forever.

At the age of twenty-one, I was married to my childhood sweetheart, although our marriage was far from sweet at the time. We had a one-year-old daughter, and I just found out I was four months along in a high-risk pregnancy.

In our minds, the last thing we needed was more complications in our life. So we discussed different options with our doctor and then elected to terminate the pregnancy. With the decision made, we set up the appointment.

When the day arrived to terminate the pregnancy, I awoke to my alarm and then proceeded to get my baby girl, Kris, ready to go to Grandma's house. This was a normal routine.

Only, that day really was not like any other day. I felt disconnected as if I was watching myself go through the motions of getting her dressed and her diaper bag packed for the day, and even as my husband and I drove her to my mother-in-law's home. But one motion after another, we kept going. We headed to the abortion clinic from there.

Approaching the parking lot, I could see people on the sidewalk holding signs that spelled, "M U R D E R."

The heaviness began to set on me as we pulled into a parking space. I felt like something was trying to tell me to not go through with it. I just shook it off and entered the facility.

Upon walking into the building, I could feel that it was void of warmth, and it felt like darkness and death hovered over the waiting area. A shiver ran down my spine as I signed into the clinic and received my paperwork.

The first item on the form was a request of payment for services rendered. My insurance would be paying the cost in full. So I signed by the *X* and continued filling out the form. I felt as though I signed a contract with the devil.

Nonetheless, I took my seat with the rest of the women. Unlike the waiting areas of an obstetrician's office, there were not any genuine smiles or giddy talk about babies. This was an abortion clinic—a place where people said "fetus" and "tissue" instead.

Silence filled the air, and I sat pretending to read a magazine, all the while internally a battle began to rage. It was as if two beings were fighting for my heart. One was crying out, "Just get up and walk out the door and leave!" The other reassured me, "You will get through this, just stay and see it through. You are doing the right thing. It is only your nerves. You will be fine."

The heaviness I came in with had not subsided, and I just sat under its weight seemingly unable to move until someone called my name. Then, lifelessly I watched a short video explaining what the procedure involved.

Next, a staff member gave an overview of the medical instruments that would be used during the procedure.

Finally, I had to sign a waiver that stated I would not sue if there were any complications. This should have hindered me more because *I did not* need any more complications. That is why I was there in the first place. Reluctantly, I signed the last form.

After what seemed like hours, each of us began to be called back, one by one. While waiting for my turn, I heard several women crying in the recovery room. Perhaps I was determined, but I brushed it off as just "after-pain from the procedure."

Then it was my turn. The nurse called my name and escorted me back to a room with an exam table and stirrups. She asked me to change into a hospital gown. Once dressed, the nurse hooked me up with an IV.

Next, the doctor came in. To my surprise, I recognized him. He was a doctor from my OB/GYN office. I informed him that I was a little nauseated, and he reassured me that it was normal to feel that way during these kinds of procedures. He claimed that I would feel better once finished.

Before sedating me, he informed me that it would only take a few minutes. He then began the procedure.

I felt some pressure. Then, I could hear the vacuum aspiration hose. I will never forget that sound. Or the feeling I felt when the hose turned off. My heart sank lower than any nauseated feeling could ever give me. All I could think was, *What have I done?*

It was as if someone just removed the blinders from my eyes and revealed the truth to me. But now, now it was too late. Before I knew it, I was sitting in the recovery room and given some medication to help with any pain I might experience. Then they released me. That was it. But nothing could have prepared me for what was to come.

When I came out to the car to meet my husband, he asked me how I was feeling. An overwhelming sadness subdued me, and I replied, "I feel like I just killed my baby." That was only the beginning of my downward spiral into emotional despair and emptiness.

A SAFE PLACE FOR YOUR THOUGHTS ...

How do you determine which choice to make when battling internally between two decisions? Do you rely on information or emotions? Do you allow other people to influence your decision?

_____

_____

_____

_____

_____

_____

_____

_____

_____

CHAPTER 3

Ton of Bricks

For Godly sorrow worketh repentance to
salvation not to be repented of: but the
sorrow of the world worketh death.

—2 Corinthians 7:10

On that day in the abortion clinic, the abortion doctor
took two lives. There was a physical death for my baby
and an emotional death for me. The doctor may not even
suffer any guilt for his actions. After all, his "procedure"
was perfectly legal at the time. But for me, the guilt hit
me like a ton of bricks.

From that day forward, I would carry the weight of
that decision and pay for it with agony. I would hear the
cry of a baby when no one was around. Yet I could not
tell anyone because they would think I was crazy. You

did not talk about that kind of thing in the '80s. Many times, I thought suicide would be easier than hearing a baby cry.

Then the unthinkable happened. Six months after the abortion, I became pregnant again. I began to question myself, "How could I carry another baby after I murdered my last baby? How could I possibly love this baby well enough when I did not deserve to even love or cherish a baby again?"

I did not know how I would offer my love to this baby whom I thought would one day come to reject me. But I knew one thing; no matter what, I would not abort this baby.

With this pregnancy the emotions from the abortion only became harder to control and console. With every first there was a first that I missed with the baby I aborted previously. Grief choked out each joy. The first time hearing the baby's heartbeat. The gender reveal—it's a girl! The first kick … That was an especially hard one.

Whenever I would feel her move inside of me, there was a phantom-like feeling in my womb. That is the only way I know how to describe it.

It was as if the kicks were not just those of the baby girl I was carrying but those also of my aborted baby.

I can only liken it to someone who has had a limb amputated. Occasionally and unexplainably, they can still feel sensation in the limb that is no longer present. It is often painful—not only physically but emotionally as well.

That sensation serves as a reminder of the once attached limb—once lively and full of purpose. Now, gone forever—like my baby.

When the time came to give birth to my daughter, it was eight weeks early. She had to stay in the hospital for a little while. I blamed myself for her early delivery and complications. I figured they were God's way of punishing me for the abortion.

Thankfully, however, we did get to take our baby girl home. She had quite the warrior spirit—she fought to survive, and that same spirit is still alive and well in her! We named her "Trishia Jo" after my nurse, her paternal grandpa, and my best friend, T. J.

Once we got Trishia home from the hospital, we began settling in. I had hoped that things would be different emotionally now that she was born and home safely.

But one day as I was feeding her, a voice out of nowhere whispered into my ear, "You don't deserve that beautiful baby girl. What will she think when she is older and learns the truth about the baby before her?"

In my heart, it felt as though those words had come through a megaphone. Another pile of guilt bricks dumped on me. Only this time, they built a wall.

One would have thought that I would have showered her in more love and care in efforts to make up for the abortion or to prove that whisper wrong at the very least. That was not the case though. I loved this sweet, innocent baby more than life itself, but guilt drove so many of my actions.

I would play with her and care for her physically, but emotionally I kept her at arm's length. It is not that I wanted to be that distant from her, but I had convinced myself that I did not deserve to have her or have that motherly relationship with her.

As time passed, she found someone who would be emotionally there for her. It was one of her aunts. This aunt would become the person she trusted and in whom she confided.

It was my fault that she could not do that with me. I did not see it at the time though. I just thought I was protecting us both from the inevitable heartbreak of shame and rejection that she would one day feel toward me. I was deceived. The reality is that I was giving her more reason to hurt and to be disappointed with me than if I just embraced her despite my past choice.

The years went by, and as Trish got older, we were never close like a mother and daughter should be. There was a period where we even went months without speaking.

On her wedding day, which should have been one of the happiest days between a mother and daughter, I felt unwanted. The things we did do together felt obligatory on her end. I did not even get to help her dress or put her jewelry on. I seemed to miss all the special bonding moments mothers have with their daughters on their wedding days.

Seven years later, our relationship still only held on by a thread. We talked and tried to be loving and cordial with one another. But some feelings finally surfaced after the birth of her daughter, Alexis.

As a new mother, she could not understand how I distanced myself from her all those years when she was little. She had an overwhelming love for Alexis. Shouldn't I have had the same love for her?

A SAFE PLACE FOR YOUR THOUGHTS ...

Have you ever seen the weight of your decisions poorly affect relationships with those you love, whether immediately or over time?

_____

_____

_____

_____

_____

_____

_____

_____

_____

_____

CHAPTER 4

The Dark before the Dawn

Who hath delivered us from the power of
darkness, and hath translated us into the kingdom
of his dear son: In whom we have redemption
through his blood, even the forgiveness of sin.

—Colossians 1:13–14

The answer to her question is a resounding yes! But let
me take you to the middle of my story, some twenty
years ago in December of 1997, when the enemy of my
soul was out to do more than destroy me—he was out
to kill.

After taking a few too many pills with alcohol one
night, I found myself in a psych ward at a hospital with
a therapist sitting across from me. I did not want to live
anymore.

I was tired of arguing with my husband, tired of feeling unwanted, and tired of feeling like my kids would be better off without me. I was absolutely exhausted with my battle against the shame and sorrow that came with my abortion thirteen years prior.

Straitjackets do not cure this kind of weariness, but the advice the doctor gave would not bring a cure either. When he came in, we discussed why I tried to take my own life. I told him about the arguments with my husband, and I told him about how the abortion had left me in turmoil. His advice in regard to the abortion recovery was verbatim: "You will get over it."

Perhaps he had no other words to give because he could not understand or did not know what to say. But he seemed to have a solution for my marital problems and feelings of being unwanted and not needed: "antidepressants and outpatient therapy."

With that advice, the hospital released me five days later under the care of my mother since my husband's work schedule was not compatible with my outpatient therapy.

During my therapy sessions, we addressed all the issues mentioned in the hospital, but once again the postabortion trauma seemed to go ignored. I felt alone.

After a few weeks of therapy, the kids and I left my mom's home and went back to ours.

The new year had come now, and I called one of my brothers on a Sunday morning. This brother was a Christian, and I figured he would be going to church. Nevertheless, I still asked him if he planned to go that morning. He fired back, "Yes, why, would you like to go?"

My answer was yes!

Half an hour later he was at my house ready to pick up his little sister for church! We drove a little while then pulled into the parking lot of the church he attended. The small, red brick building set just outside of a small town in the middle of nowhere.

When we went inside to the sanctuary, I noticed the white walls and that the mauve carpet matched the padded pews. I met the pastor—a friendly, gray-haired man. He was short like me, maybe five feet four.

His congregation was very warm and friendly, but I cannot recall the sermon he preached, nor can I recall the names of the songs that he led that day. But I do remember a peculiar experience that would get my attention and keep it forever.

While the choir was singing, I was skimming through

the red-back hymnal when I stopped on a page and began to read it. Then, suddenly the pastor stopped the choir midsong. He said the Lord impressed on him to go to another page instead.

The page happened to be the same page that I was on! Call it strange once maybe. But then it happened two more times during worship and again when he preached! I could not wrap my brain around it, so I tried to shrug it off as coincidence.

For the rest of the day, I kept replaying that morning in my head, trying to make sense of it all. Later that afternoon though, I could not shake it anymore! It was eating at me. I needed to know if it was a coincidence or not. Finally, I called my brother and asked if I could ride with him again to the evening service. He agreed, and we went.

I could not deny the working of God if I wanted to—the same exact thing happened again that night! I had never experienced anything like it before. The Lord revealed himself to me that day through those experiences, and before that service was over, I was down on my knees at the altar, and I accepted Jesus into my heart.

The enemy had left me for dead, but Jesus saw

something worth saving in those dead ashes, and he breathed life into me in a whole new way.

It had been a little over a month since I went home and a month since I received salvation when another tempestuous thing happened.

When I stepped out of my front door to go to church, I lost my footing on the ice. When I tried to stand, the pain in my ankle was so unbearable that I thought I would pass out. So I called for an ambulance, and the paramedics drove me to the hospital.

The news at the hospital was not good. I had crushed my ankle and needed to have surgery, so they admitted me. I had screws and pins put in the next morning. Upon release, the doctor gave strict orders not to put pressure of any kind on my ankle for eight weeks. Once again, I had to stay at my mother's home so that I could have help.

At a follow-up appointment, I was disappointed to find that the pins were slipping, and another surgery was necessary, prolonging my time away from home and my husband even more. So my two daughters and I stayed with my mother for an additional eight weeks, which did not do any favors for my marriage.

Finally, I was strong enough to be on crutches, and

the girls and I headed home. From there, I continued to blaze a new path although spiritually and physically it felt a little more like a hobble. It was hard. But it was worth it, and I was grateful for this new life!

Unfortunately, the arguing between my husband and me did not get better because "I found Jesus." In fact, things only seemed to get worse.

After fourteen years of marriage, a fourteen-year-old daughter named Kristine, an aborted child, and a twelve-year-old daughter named Trishia, we let go of our union. I was leaving behind so much pain and suffering. But the one thing I desperately wanted to let go of was the guilt of that abortion. It seemed nearly impossible.

A SAFE PLACE FOR YOUR THOUGHTS ...

I know my experience with the Lord that day is one that no one could take away from me. Have you ever experienced something so surreal that you knew it was not coincidence? Explain.

_____

_____

_____

_____

_____

_____

_____

_____

CHAPTER 5

Rug. Run. Rescue. Rest.

Come unto me, all ye that labor and are heavy
laden, and I will give you rest. Take my yoke upon
you, and learn of me; for I am meek and lowly in
heart: and ye shall find rest unto your souls.

—Matthew 11:28–29

With a broken family, a young faith, and a hope for the
future, I charged ahead.

Surface level, I tried to hide my bondage to guilt,
shame, and fear, but it was like a bad stain in the carpet.
You know the kind. You keep scrubbing it, but it keeps
returning so you end up covering it with a rug.

So that is what I did; I swept my problems under the
rug. That is, until someone swept me off my feet.

Not long after my divorce, I married a wonderful

Christian man that attended my brother's church, which had also become my home church.

We exchanged vows there in that little red brick church with my two daughters present and his three children. He had two daughters and a son. Now, together, we had four daughters, one son, and the shadow of a child that should have been there.

We were now a blended family, which comes with its own challenges naturally. But I loved this man named Jim and his dimples that made my heart skip a beat. His six-foot, well-built stature, next to my five-foot-three frame didn't look quite perfect, but it felt perfect.

As his wife, I found my new role to be exciting but challenging. He served in ministry, and with being saved only a little over a year and dealing with a past that still haunted me, I felt completely inadequate for this task.

Pretty soon it felt like my happy face rug covering my stain got a snag.

Then each time something happened, it became a little more frayed, unravelling more and more of my hidden pain and bitterness. One of the hardest tears occurred when our son, Bryant, drowned under someone else's care. Now I had lost two children—one by my own choice, and one that was not of my own choosing.

Time would go on, and so would the fraying.

Fear gripped me at the forefront of being a minister's wife. My husband was an amazing preacher, spiritually mature, and a prayer warrior. I thought I could handle being a part of the ministry at first. But I was battling a demon underneath that frayed rug, and I had allowed it to convince me that there was no place in ministry for a woman that had an abortion.

So I ran. I ran before the frayed rug would run out of thread. I ran before my stain could be exposed. I ran from my husband. I ran from my kids. I ran from the ministry. I ran from a baby that would not let me forget what I had done, and I ran from God.

One day I just got in my car and left everyone and everything behind—not because I wanted to intentionally hurt anyone. But because once again, I did not think I was worthy of anyone or anything. However, I found that I could not outrun the love and mercy of God.

He revealed his love and mercy to me in a deeper way than previously experienced. He showed me his character through my husband. Hours after leaving, I called my husband. He did not greet me with an angry voice or malice; instead, I was met with a soft word and love—two things I did not deserve.

My husband said that he just wanted me to come home and try to fix whatever was wrong. To be frank, in my mind I was screaming, "A doctor cannot fix me; God cannot fix me; no one can fix me!" But I knew I had to decide to stop running and to face my demons, which were ashes of my past. I knew I had to get help. No more rug. No more running. I was being rescued.

I went back home to a man that had more patience than any man I have ever known. He had shown me pure love that day. It was a love I had never felt before. It was an agape love. I was finally able to deal with my ashes.

Immediately, I began counseling with a professional Christian counselor and our pastor. I vividly recall the day when I surrendered all the hurt, pain, guilt, and shame to Christ. I felt Jesus in that room, and my tears flowed like a river pouring out of me. I began to feel something that I had not felt in years—peace. I felt peace wash over me, and I could feel God's love surround me. It was as if he opened his arms and wrapped me up in a big hug as only a father could do, and he spoke these words into my spirit: "Rest, my child."

There it was: rest from my running and rest from my

weariness of carrying the weight of this sin for so many years.

Finally, I could receive that forgiveness that I had closed myself off to all these years. God broke the chains of depression, guilt, shame, and condemnation that Satan had placed on me. I learned to truly forgive myself and gained peace with God.

That Mother's Day, God emboldened me to share my testimony with my church family.

Though it may seem like a twisted testimony to share on such a day, it spoke measures of my God's redeeming power. He took this sinner mother and made her free. But that was just the beginning.

A SAFE PLACE FOR YOUR THOUGHTS ...

What is your greatest memory of feeling acceptance? Alternatively, what is your saddest memory of feeling rejected? How have you dealt with both of those memories?

_____

_____

_____

_____

_____

_____

_____

_____

CHAPTER 6

Redeemed Relationships

Let the redeemed of the LORD say so, whom he
hath redeemed from the hand of the enemy.

—Psalm 107:2

Although I finally had this amazing newfound peace
and rest, there were still so many details to work out. The
aftermath of an abortion is far more than forgiveness
from Christ and self.

People all around me needed understanding and
healing too. My relationships with people needed
mending, and it would take the Lord to bring life where
there had been ashes.

My husband has been the one who suffered through
with me, never forsaking me, even when at times I know

it would have been easier than dealing with me, I am sure. But he held on.

Now he rejoices with me, knowing that God has done a profound thing in my heart and in our lives. He has watched God transform me inside out. I am forever grateful for his consistent prayer and patience.

My relationship with my daughters took different turns at different times. One daughter could not understand why she did not feel loved, and another daughter had followed in my footsteps of abortion, self-destruction, and running. But God did not allow those relationships to be severed forever! Praise the Lord!

The daughter that could not understand our strained relationship received counsel to deal with the emotions and feelings she experienced. Then, when the time was right, she approached me with the way she felt. I finally came clean with my own feelings, and we finally began to understand one another.

After much hard work, the process of healing began. We are still healing, but we have a new relationship in light of the truth and love, not motivated by guilt. We are finally having some of those longed-for mother-daughter moments. To God be all the glory!

The daughter that walked in my footsteps began

taking those steps during my guilt-stained days. So when I received the phone call, I heaped even more guilt onto my weary soul. I felt responsible for the abortion of my child and grandchild because I felt that my choices paved the way for my daughter.

As time continued, I noticed patterns in her life that were distinctively familiar to me. I hurt for her. But until I received healing, I did not know how to help her. She knew my experience and my shame, but she never knew my healing. So she too embraced the lie and ran like I did.

Thankfully, however, she is beginning to face her ashes too. Only she can tell her story, and maybe one day that will come. But right now, as a mother who understands both the weight of sin and the freedom of forgiveness, I am walking in truth with my daughter, praying for her to look to the one who set me free and will do the same for her. I know so much beauty is ahead!

My relationship has evolved with my other two daughters as well. Even though I didn't give birth to them, they experienced my hardness over the years, and they have also witnessed the softness that has come through my peace and freedom in the Lord! We too are bonding in ways we never could before! I am so grateful!

Relationships outside of my family have taken a different shape as well. No longer am I hiding behind shame, but I carry confidence in what Christ has done for me. He redeemed me.

A SAFE PLACE FOR YOUR THOUGHTS ...

Have you ever seen God's grace come in unexpected ways? I never realized that my personal journey of healing would lead to a restored relationship with my family, but I am so grateful it did. List a few relationships that you know you need God's help in restoring. Then pray over them.

_____

_____

_____

_____

_____

_____

_____

_____

CHAPTER 7

My Story Is Not Hers

I will instruct thee and teach thee in the way which
thou shalt go: I will guide thee with mine eye.

—Psalm 32:8

So that is the story I told the young woman on the other
end of that phone, only in not so many words.

Of course, I also could not tell her word-for-word
what my family members experienced over time. But
what I was able to do was relate with her fears, share my
experience, and express to her how much this decision
would affect the rest of her life and every relationship
from this moment on—for good or bad.

I needed her to know that ending her pregnancy
or continuing her pregnancy would not resolve her

problems and that the aftermath of abortion is nothing less than feelings of guilt, shame, and emptiness.

I also desperately needed her to understand that she was not just addressing her future; she was determining the future of another life.

As I finished sharing my story with her, I advised her to have an ultrasound. As much as I do not agree with making feeling-based decisions when it comes to life, I told her to do just that, in high hopes she would choose wisely.

I told her, "Go have an ultrasound, pay attention to the monitor, and listen closely to the sound of the heartbeat. If the slightest tug pulls at your heart, continue your pregnancy and have your baby. But if you truly do not believe you are carrying a baby, then do what you feel is best and live your life with no regrets."

We continued to text a little throughout the rest of the night, and I let her know that my husband and I would be praying for her.

When we finished texting, I placed my phone on the nightstand. Then, in that moment, the Lord showed me that I was enough and that he was using what the enemy meant for harm to be a help to someone else. I realized that sometimes it takes someone that has been there and lived through the darkness to shine the brightest in someone else's midnight hour.

For the next four and a half weeks, my husband and I prayed and fasted for her and the unborn baby until we finally received word from her one day going into the fifth week. I received a picture of an ultrasound with a text.

It was good news! She chose life! She thanked me for being there for her, for sharing my story, and for shining a bright light into her dark hour.

That was not my light though; that was the light of Christ shining through me to spare her and her child. My God did the remarkable. He took a text message and turned it into life intervention! He took a text message and turned it into a victory! He took a text message and turned it into redemption!

That day I truly felt redeemed. Thirty-four years ago, two souls died in an abortion clinic—one physically and one emotionally—all because of one choice that I made. But by God's grace, these many years later, God chose to use me, because I simply chose to answer his call. He used my ashes to spare two lives! I will never forget the experience from that night.

I do not believe this young woman will ever forget

either, as she now calls that little baby from the ultrasound picture her daughter. That little girl is almost seven years old, and I am most certain that God has a beautiful plan for her life. As for her mommy, she still got to fulfill her dream of participating in New York Fashion Week and is raising her sweet little one with great joy!

As the Lord prompts me, I share this story with others. It is not to gloat over myself or to tear anyone down but to simply share that God is aware of our every circumstance and he cares. He is a life-giving, life-saving, and life-altering God!

He showed up in my darkness.

He showed up at my brick wall.

He showed up under my rug.

He showed up when I ran.

He showed up when I came home.

He showed up when I faced it all.

He showed up for that young woman and he will show up for you too. He can bring life where death abounds and give us beauty for our ashes. When the way may seem uncertain and lonely, he is ready to show us the path in which to walk and to guide us.

A SAFE PLACE FOR YOUR THOUGHTS ...

Have you ever experienced a moment when you have truly felt redeemed? Describe that moment or feeling.

_____

_____

_____

_____

_____

_____

_____

_____

_____

CHAPTER 8

Known

Before I formed thee in the belly, I knew thee.

—Jeremiah 1:5

As precious as it is to me that Christ was with me in all those undeserving times, I have now given him the reigns to be so much more than just present in my life. He is the Lord of my life, and I am convinced that through him my healing continues. It did not stop at one profound moment, but rather I have had healing heaped upon healing!

He is constantly making all things new. I am sure to experience the Father's great love and unending mercy always, and for that I am eternally grateful. However, I believe part of my healing has not come through coming to terms with my abortion, receiving forgiveness, fortifying my relationships, or helping others through their darkness.

No, part of my healing has been in bringing some sort of restitution to my little baby that I aborted. I knew the least that I could give my child was acknowledgment—not as just the aborted baby but as my baby.

A mother does not hurt over a baby she never loved. But I am a mother that chose wrongly under the impression that I was doing the right thing, as many other mothers have done.

Today, many women are deceived. Like me, doctors tell them that pregnancies are optional. Essentially my pregnancy had more to do with my rights and privileges over my body than the rights of any preborn baby.

High-risk pregnancy for many doctors means that you forfeit the most vulnerable, which in this case would be the little life dependent on my womb to survive. The ideology behind this is completely nonmaternal. But it is also selfish.

At the time I could not see it as being selfish or unloving, as I am sure many others are blind to these truths too. But this is because of the ill-taught belief that babies in the womb are merely masses of tissue and dispensable—or that it would be more humane to murder than to let them live a possibly limited lifestyle with disabilities or hardships.

There truly are so many lies out there and pressure from people to make decisions that are convenient—or appear to be right. Such was the case with me. I thought the doctor knew best, and I thought it convenient to avoid a complicated, life-threatening pregnancy.

However, if I could take back that choice—to preserve the life of my child, to fight through every day of that pregnancy—I would do it. Why?

Because I knew the instant that abortionist took my baby from me that it was truly my baby—not a ball of tissue or a problem child. My heart hurt as only a mother could hurt. I grieved over that choice—that sin—as only a mother could grieve.

So to the same extent that I have grieved as a mother, I want to acknowledge my baby's memory and life with honor, dignity, and love.

Nine years ago, around the time of the anniversary of the abortion, I came across a website that recommended naming your aborted baby. I had never thought to do that, and I thought it was a wonderful way to give honor to my baby.

I knew that my baby was a boy. So I gave him the

name that I would have given him if he had born to me—Anthony, named after his daddy. I know that may sound a little crazy considering I am no longer married to his father. But despite my relationship with his father now, I know that would have been my choice for him then, being that he would have been the firstborn son.

And even though I named him after his earthly father; my little guy has the likeness of his heavenly Father—perfection. His life, though short lived here, continues in the presence of the Lord, where he can embrace the Father's love and, one day, mine.

Until then, I will continue to be grateful for the impact his life has had on mine and many others. God has allowed his life to be full of purpose. He did not allow for the enemy to snuff out his calling because of me. Instead, God is using that horrible experience to spare the lives of many other Anthonys.

And while etymologists debate whether the name Anthony means "praiseworthy" or "flower," it is my understanding that it means both.

Because of Anthony, I met Jesus. Had I not felt the weight of sin or carried the burden of guilt from the abortion, I would have never come to the place where I would surrender all.

Christ did the unthinkable. In exchange for all my suicidal thoughts, all my pain, and all my wickedness, he gave me salvation, rest for my soul, and a promise to one day see my baby in heaven. That sounds like life after death—as if God allowed a rose to blossom among my ashes. He is worthy of all my praise!

My boy deserved more than a name and a place in my heart, though; he deserved a place in our family.

Throughout the years, I have wondered who he would be. Would he be bashful like his older sister or have a bolder personality like me and his little sister? Would he have auburn, wavy hair and green eyes like Kris? Or maybe big brown eyes and brown hair like Trishia?

I cannot tell whether I would still have my family now or if my ex-husband and I would have made things work because I cannot predict what Anthony's birth or the absence of Trishia could bring. But if everything else remained the same as it is now, he would have met Jim, his little sisters, and his little brother. I have often wondered if he and Bryant would have been close.

Interestingly, he would have come to have a brother-in-law named Anthony too. Out of all the things he could have been—a doctor, a mechanic, a preacher, or a singer—I would have been happy to have him be a good, God-fearing young man like my son-in-law, because while he is no replacement, I do feel like he was a godsend to our family.

Of course, the questions and what-ifs keep coming, but they will go unanswered for now. No longer, though, will my baby Anthony go on unnoticed because of my shame. It was not his fault that he is not here, and his sisters deserve to love him just as they loved their brother Bryant.

But how does one hold a memory of someone they never met? I suppose one really cannot do that, but one can acknowledge his or her existence and value.

I feel as if the Lord gave me a way to do just that—one more way to bring some sort of restitution to my son and his life.

One evening while I was sitting on the couch in our family room and looking at our beautiful Christmas tree, the Lord began to speak to me about placing an ornament on the tree for Anthony.

Our tree had ornaments from each of our children and grandchildren, except for Anthony. Because he never experienced a Christmas with us, it never occurred to me that I should place an ornament on the tree for him. But the purpose behind this direction from the Lord was not so much about the tree itself or even a specific ornament. It was about acknowledging my son and his place in our lives. His memory did not need to live on only in an abortion statistic or in my regrets but rightfully as my beloved child that I so desperately wanted to have with me, just as I wanted our son Bryant with us again.

Grateful for the gentle leading of the Lord, I headed to my nearest Hobby Lobby in search of the perfect ornament. I did not know what to get, but I knew that when I saw the one, I would know it.

Once at the store, I checked all over where they keep the single ornaments, and nothing stood out. As I rounded a corner, though, I saw the most beautiful pair of angel wings sparkling in front of me. This was the one.

When the time came to place his ornament on the tree, I stood with blurred vision, trying to look through tear-filled eyes, for the perfect spot.

Then I saw it. As I placed his ornament on the tree, I closed my eyes and asked the Lord to give my baby boy a hug and to tell him that Mommy loved him. He may not have come home in the way he deserved, but he did now have a place on our Christmas tree and within our family forever.

When I see those angel wings, I will think of Anthony being safe under the wings of his heavenly Father amid an angelic choir giving God praise for his marvelous works. But I will also think of how one day I will get to join him and tell him how much I love him face-to-face—to know him as I have so desperately longed for and to be known by him as simply "Mom," thanks to the redeeming power of Christ Jesus.

This is a picture of the angel wings ornament I placed on my tree in honor of baby Anthony.

A SAFE PLACE FOR YOUR THOUGHTS ...

Is there someone in your life that you have neglected to honor? Maybe you have overlooked someone or taken them for granted? Or, maybe you just did not know what to do. Take some time now to think of a way to honor someone you care about—whether it is a parent, a friend, or even your own aborted child.

_____

_____

_____

_____

_____

_____

_____

_____

CHAPTER 9

Freedom

Then they cried unto the LORD in their trouble,
and he saved them out of their distresses. He
brought them out of darkness and the shadow
of death, and break their bands in sunder.

—Psalm 107:13–14

A letter from my heart to you.

Dear Friend,

I hope you do not mind me calling you friend. But I feel
like maybe me divulging some of my deepest, darkest
secrets and some of my greatest joys with you has given
me some room to call you friend. If not, I apologize. Just
think of me calling you stranger; after all, I have had

pretty good success in talking to complete strangers. (I hope you got the joke there).

But really, can I just share my heart with you? Fear, shame, and guilt had me bound for many years before I was brave enough to ask for help.

Some parts of my life might have been different if I had searched sooner, but God has allowed my brokenness to lead to a path with purpose. In sharing my story with others, I hope to be an instrument in their journey of healing and understanding.

Maybe you are not a woman who has suffered the heartache after abortion. Maybe you are a family member who has sat on the sidelines helplessly watching. Or maybe you yourself are an abortionist or an advocate for abortion. Perhaps you are a survivor of abortion. I do not know who you are, but I know that you are not reading this book for mere pleasure.

God has orchestrated this place in time for you— whether it is for you to heal personally or to pass along to someone you know. But it is not by coincidence any more than those hymns sung on the day I gave my life to Christ were by coincidence.

So no matter who you are or what your circumstances

are, please do not miss this moment. It is bigger than my story.

What is God speaking to you right now? Do you have unforgiveness in your heart? Is fear gripping you? Are you running? Do you feel alone? Are you in need of healing? Are you in the middle of making a hard decision? If you are saying yes to any of those questions, I encourage you to ask for help.

I know firsthand that the most important relationship I had to establish was the one with Jesus Christ. But what I found is that while I accepted that he could forgive me, I did not allow myself to believe that anyone else could—not even myself.

So I allowed fear, guilt, and shame to rule my heart instead of allowing God's love and mercy to permeate it. Those things overflowed into all my relationships and left them in ruins. I am here to tell you that you do not have to let this happen or continue to happen to you! There is freedom!

If you have been reading the scripture at the beginning of each chapter, then you probably will recognize the following verse:

> Then they cried unto the LORD in their
> trouble, and he saved them out of their
> distresses. He brought them out of darkness
> and the shadow of death, and break their
> bands in sunder. (Psalm 107:13–14)

This verse says that when people cried unto the Lord in their trouble he saved them out of it and brought them out of their darkness and broke their chains; that's exactly what God did for me, and he can do it for you.

I implore you today to call on the name of the Lord above everything else! But then I plead with you to please talk to someone else too!

As I mentioned at the very beginning of this book, we each have an intricate part in the kingdom of God, if we will walk in it. Our placement is not based just upon bringing God glory, though. He created us with qualities and skill sets that we would need in each other. We strengthen and edify one another to build up the kingdom of God. There is no shame in seeking help from someone else, and if someone has told you otherwise, I am so sorry!

Just saying yes to one of those questions lets me know

that you have some acknowledgment, and you are ready to begin to live again. It is time for the next step.

Maybe you will reach out to a pastor or to a Christian counselor like I did. Maybe you have an understanding spouse. Maybe you do not have any of those people in your life. Do not get discouraged. I have also included some resources and scriptures in the back of this book to help you. Pray and ask the Lord to lead you in choosing someone to walk alongside you.

If you are a woman like me who has had an abortion, I would like to refer you to one of the many support groups available. Many agencies have abortion recovery groups led by women who themselves have experienced abortion. These groups offer you a safe, confidential, and nonjudgmental environment.

Some groups meet one on one; others meet in a group setting. Either way, they provide a positive setting for you to receive help.

Typically, these groups allow individuals to share their stories or to simply listen to what others have to say. The people present understand the emotions you are experiencing because they themselves have experienced it.

Some are faith-based, and some are not, but they all have one goal, and that is for you to have peace in your mind, forgiveness in your heart, and rest for your soul. Isn't that what we all want? I truly believe so, even if it is hard to admit.

Writing about my experiences was the last thing I ever dreamed of doing. It was a very private matter. But while writing, I have found that God brought even more healing to me and my family. I never imagined having the freedom that I have now, but it has been life changing!

Since the inception of this book, God has also opened doors for me to minister locally to the needs of women right here in my own neighborhood. He provided a way for me to meet every week, at the local Birthright, with women who have had abortions.

I am continuously seeing God work despite my past, and I know he has a work to do in your life too. There is a rose among the ashes.

Sincerely,
Tamara Webb

A SAFE PLACE FOR YOUR THOUGHTS ...

If you reached out for help today, what would you say?
Likewise, if someone reached out to you for help, how
would you guide them? Remember, we were meant to
help each other.

_____

_____

_____

_____

_____

_____

_____

_____

FROM MOTHER TO MOM:
ONE DAUGHTER'S PERSPECTIVE

And he that sat upon the throne said, "Behold,
I make all things new. And he said unto me,
Write: for these words are true and faithful."

—Revelation 21:5

My daughter Trishia wrote the following to help you
better understand, from her perspective, how my abortion
affected her. I believe this is an important aspect of my
story because it is a reminder that our lives are woven
together, and our choices do affect others.

I am the child after an abortion. I am grateful that
my parents decided to keep me. My mother had an
abortion in between my oldest sister and myself. You
would not think that children could be affected by
someone else's choice to have an abortion, but they can.
This is my story.

Growing up I never felt loved by my mother. I always questioned why. I never was able to build that special bond between a mother and daughter. I remember longing for her love, always asking myself why she liked other children more than myself. Why wouldn't she let me love her. *Why?*

There was one special person in my life, my aunt, that gave me a mother's love that I never knew existed. I clung to her; I always wanted to be with her. She gave me precious memories with her from a young age to my teenage years. She inspired me to be a gracious young lady and taught me how to care for others.

My parents divorced when I was twelve. During the process I overheard my mother tell my dad she did not want me. Now, at the time I did not understand her reasoning. I was devastated. I would not speak to her for about two years.

My dad raised me as a single father other than for a short stint of time where I did live with my mother and her new family at sixteen. I later moved out of state with my dad.

I could never build relationships with women and struggle to this day because the only one I ever wanted to have a relationship with was not there. I was always scared to even build friendships because I just assumed they would leave me or that I was not good enough. This led to a lonely life.

At twenty-three, I gave birth to a beautiful baby girl. Once life settled with having a newborn, I began having an awakening. I had memories coming back and feelings I could not understand. I could not comprehend how a mother could be so distant and unloving toward her child.

For years, I tried to build a relationship with her, and it always failed. I felt all alone. I felt unwanted. Not good enough. I still doubt to this day that I am worthy enough or good enough. I had no one to help me understand what it meant to be a mother—what to do, how to do it—and it was so hard. I sought counseling, and it only got worse.

For thirty years I prayed that God would break the hold on my mother's heart. That one day, just one day, I could understand why. Why I was never put first and why could she just not love me and want to be with me.

When I was thirty, my mother began experiencing a spiritual breakthrough. She was working on this book you are reading now and reliving her emotions over an abortion she had over thirty-three years ago.

As we spoke from time to time about the book, she would express some of the emotions she was going through. Then one day, I got a call from her. When I answered all I heard was sobbing, and then she said, "I hope you know I love you and always have. I have not always shown or expressed it to you because I didn't know how, but I love you."

With her first sentence out, I began to roll my eyes. But then she expanded. She told me her story, which you just read, about an abortion that she had before I was born and how it affected her and how it bled into our relationship.

From that day on, we began talking every morning and multiple times a day—sharing our days and stories of our life.

Now at thirty-three, I can call her mom. I never called her mom before this time. It was always *mother*. The word *mother* to me meant the woman who gave birth to me and that was it. Calling her *mom* meant a step closer to that relationship that I desired so heavily to have.

A SAFE PLACE FOR YOUR THOUGHTS ...

If someone has deeply hurt you, do seek understanding, but do not neglect forgiveness. Sometimes we will never understand why others do what they do. But please do not live the rest of your life harboring unforgiveness or doubting your value because of the actions of another. Christ set the perfect example for us in that while we were still sinners, he died for us. Take the time now to give God praise for his example of sacrificial love and great mercy!

_____

_____

_____

_____

_____

_____

RESOURCES

Concepts of Truth International

24/7 confidential help for grief and loss after abortion.

1-866-482-LIFE

internationalhelpline.org

Birthright International

24/7 confidential help and support to women.

1-800-550-4900

birthright.org

Freedom Ministry

Abortion Recovery

1-937-733-7743

birthright.org/eaton

SCRIPTURES

The following pages are here for you to
reference when you are needing help with:

Faith

Fear

Forgiveness

Guilt

Help in Troubles

Hope

God's Love

Peace

Repentance

Salvation

Shame

Freedom from Sin

Redemption from Sin

FAITH

As ye have therefore received Christ Jesus the Lord, so walk ye in him: Rooted and built up in him, and stablished in the faith, as ye have been taught, abounding therein with thanksgiving. (Colossians 2:6–7)

For by grace are ye saved through faith; and that not of yourselves: it is the gift of God. (Ephesians 2:8)

For we walk by faith, not by sight. (2 Corinthians 5:7)

Wherefore seeing we also are compassed about with so great a cloud of witnesses, let us lay aside every weight, and the sin which doth so easily beset us, and let us run with patience the race that is set before us.

Looking unto Jesus the author and finisher of our faith; who for the joy that was set before him endured the cross, despising the shame, and is set down at the right hand of the throne of God. (Hebrews 12:1–2)

FEAR

For I the LORD thy God will hold thy right hand, saying unto thee, Fear not; I will help thee. (Isaiah 41:13)

For God hath not given us the spirit of fear; but of power, and of love, and of a sound mind. (2 Timothy 1:7)

And it shall come to pass in the day that the LORD shall give thee rest from thy sorrow, and from thy fear, and from the hard bondage wherein thou wast made to serve. (Isaiah 14:3)

For ye have not received the spirit of bondage again to fear; but ye have received the Spirit of adoption, whereby we cry, Abba, Father. (Romans 8:15)

So that we may boldly say, The Lord is my helper, and I will not fear what man shall do unto me. (Hebrews 13:6)

FORGIVENESS

And when ye stand praying, forgive, if ye have ought against any: that your Father also which is in heaven may forgive you your trespasses. But if ye do not forgive, neither will your Father which is in heaven forgive your trespasses. (Mark 11:25–26)

For if ye forgive men their trespasses, your heavenly Father will also forgive you. (Matthew 6:14)

Be ye therefore merciful, as your Father also is merciful. Judge not, and ye shall not be judged: condemn not, and ye shall not be condemned: forgive, and ye shall be forgiven: Give, and it shall be given unto you; good measure, pressed down, and shaken together, and running over, shall men give into your bosom. For with the same measure that ye mete withal it shall be measured to you again. (Luke 6:36–38)

GUILT

If we confess our sins, he is faithful and just to forgive us our sins, and to cleanse us from all unrighteousness. (1 John 1:9)

For if our heart condemns us, God is greater than our heart, and knoweth all things. (1 John 3:20)

Therefore, if any man be in Christ, he is a new creature: old things are passed away; behold, all things are become new. (2 Corinthians 5:17)

And they shall teach no more every man his neighbor, and every man his brother, saying, Know the LORD: for they shall all know me, from the least of them unto the greatest of them, saith the LORD: for I will forgive their iniquity, and I will remember their sin no more. (Jeremiah 31:34)

I write unto you, little children, because your sins are forgiven you for his name's sake. (1 John 2:12)

HELP IN TROUBLES

The LORD is good, a strong hold in the day of trouble; and he knoweth them that trust in him. (Nahum 1:7)

My flesh and my heart faileth: but God is the strength of my heart, and my portion forever. (Psalm 73:26)

The LORD is my strength and my shield; my heart trusted in him, and I am helped: therefore, my heart greatly rejoiceth; and with my song will I praise him. (Psalm 28:7)

The LORD is my rock, and my fortress, and my deliverer; my God, my strength, in whom I will trust; my buckler, and the horn of my salvation, and my high tower. (Psalm 18:2)

These things I have spoken unto you, that in me ye might have peace. In the world ye shall have tribulation: but be of good cheer; I have overcome the world. (John 16:33)

HOPE

Why art thou cast down, O my soul? and why art thou disquieted within me? hope thou in God: for I shall yet praise him, who is the health of my countenance, and my God. (Psalm 42:11)

Who by him do believe in God, that raised him up from the dead, and gave him glory; that your faith and hope might be in God. (1 Peter 1:21)

Wherefore gird up the loins of your mind, be sober, and hope to the end for the grace that is to be brought unto you at the revelation of Jesus Christ. (1 Peter 1:13)

And every man that hath this hope in him purifieth himself, even as he is pure. (1 John 3:3)

Be of good courage, and he shall strengthen your heart, all ye that hope in the LORD. (Psalm 31:24)

GOD'S LOVE

For God so loved the world, that he gave his only begotten Son, that whosoever believeth in him should not perish, but have everlasting life. (John 3:16)

The LORD openeth the eyes of the blind: the LORD raiseth them that are bowed down: the LORD loveth the righteous. (Psalm 146:8)

Herein is love, not that we loved God, but that he loved us, and sent his Son to be the propitiation for our sins. (1 John 4:10)

I will heal their backsliding; I will love them freely: for mine anger is turned away from him. (Hosea 14:4)

The LORD hath appeared of old unto me, saying, Yea, I have loved thee with an everlasting love: therefore, with lovingkindness have I drawn thee. (Jeremiah 31:3)

We love him, because he first loved us. (1 John 4:19)

PEACE

I create the fruit of the lips; Peace, peace to him that is far off, and to him that is near, saith the LORD; and I will heal him. (Isaiah 57:19)

And let the peace of God rule in your hearts, to the which also ye are called in one body; and be ye thankful. (Colossians 3:15)

And the peace of God, which passeth all understanding, shall keep your hearts and minds through Christ Jesus. (Philippians 4:7)

And he said to the woman, "Thy faith hath saved thee; go in peace." (Luke 7:50)

Peace I leave with you, my peace I give unto you: not as the world giveth, give I unto you. Let not your heart be troubled, neither let it be afraid. (John 14:27)

REPENTANCE

And saying, "The time is fulfilled, and the kingdom of God is at hand: repent ye, and believe the gospel." (Mark 1:15)

The LORD is nigh unto them that are of a broken heart; and saveth such as be of a contrite spirit. (Psalm 34:18)

Repent ye therefore, and be converted, that your sins may be blotted out, when the times of refreshing shall come from the presence of the Lord. (Acts 3:19)

But if the wicked will turn from all his sins that he hath committed, and keep all my statutes, and do that which is lawful and right, he shall surely live, he shall not die. All his transgressions that he hath committed, they shall not be mentioned unto him: in his righteousness that he hath done he shall live. (Ezekiel 18:21–22)

SALVATION

For he hath made him to be sin for us, who knew no sin; that we might be made the righteousness of God in him. (2 Corinthians 5:21)

But after that the kindness and love of God our Saviour toward man appeared, not by works of righteousness which we have done, but according to his mercy he saved us, by the washing of regeneration, and renewing of the Holy Ghost; Which he shed on us abundantly through Jesus Christ our Saviour. (Titus 3:4–6)

But as many as received him, to them gave he power to become the sons of God, even to them that believe on his name: Which were born, not of blood, nor of the will of the flesh, nor of the will of man, but of God. (John 1:12–13)

SHAME

For the scripture saith, "Whosoever believeth on him shall not be ashamed." (Romans 10:11)

And hope maketh not ashamed; because the love of God is shed abroad in our hearts by the Holy Ghost which is given unto us. (Romans 5:5)

For the which cause I also suffer these things: nevertheless I am not ashamed: for I know whom I have believed, and am persuaded that he is able to keep that which I have committed unto him against that day. (2 Timothy 1:12)

Study to shew thyself approved unto God, a workman that needeth not to be ashamed, rightly dividing the word of truth. (2 Timothy 2:15)

Yet if any man suffer as a Christian, let him not be ashamed; but let him glorify God on this behalf. (1 Peter 4:16)

FREEDOM FROM SIN

Then will I sprinkle clean water upon you, and ye shall be clean: from all your filthiness, and from all your idols, will I cleanse you. A new heart also will I give you, and a new spirit will I put within you: and I will take away the stony heart out of your flesh, and I will give you a heart of flesh. (Ezekiel 36:25–26)

Knowing this, that our old man is crucified with him, that the body of sin might be destroyed, that henceforth we should not serve sin. For he that is dead is freed from sin. (Romans 6:6–7)

For sin shall not have dominion over you: for ye are not under the law, but under grace. (Romans 6:14)

REDEMPTION FROM SIN

This is a faithful saying, and worthy of all acceptation, that Christ Jesus came into the world to save sinners; of whom I am chief. (1 Timothy 1:15)

In whom we have redemption through his blood, the forgiveness of sins, according to the riches of his grace. (Ephesians 1:7)

So, Christ was once offered to bear the sins of many; and unto them that look for him shall he appear the second time without sin unto salvation. (Hebrews 9:28)

Being justified freely by his grace through the redemption that is in Christ Jesus. (Romans 3:24)

And when these things begin to come to pass, then look up, and lift up your heads; for your redemption draweth nigh. (Luke 21:28)

Printed in the United States
By Bookmasters